The TRIANGLE SHIRTWAIST

FACTORY FIRE

and the

Fight for Workers' Rights

BY JULIE GILBERT

ILLUSTRATED BY JÁNOS ORBÁN

CONSULTANT:
JAMES DIMOCK,
PROFESSOR OF COMMUNICATION STUDIES
MINNESOTA STATE UNIVERSITY, MANKATO

CAPSTONE PRESS
a capstone imprint

Graphic Library is published by Capstone Press, an imprint of Capstone.
1710 Roe Crest Drive
North Mankato, Minnesota 56003
www.capstonepub.com

Library of Congress Cataloging-in-Publication Data is available on the Library of Congress website.

ISBN: 978-1-4966-8120-1 (library binding)
ISBN: 978-1-4966-8688-6 (paperback)
ISBN: 978-1-4966-8157-7 (eBook PDF)

Summary: In November 1909, thousands of factory workers walked off the job to protest terrible working conditions in New York City factories. Joining the picket lines was dangerous, but the protests stirred action. Some factory owners finally agreed to improve conditions, but nothing changed for workers at the Triangle Shirtwaist Factory. Those workers paid a high price for the company's dangerous conditions in 1911, when a deadly fire swept through the Triangle factory. How did this tragedy embolden the fight for workers' rights?

Editorial Credits
Editor: Julie Gassman; Designer: Tracy McCabe;
Media Researcher: Eric Gohl; Production Specialist: Laura Manthe

Design Elements
Shutterstock: Alted Studio, 2, 3, 28–32 (background), Mika Shysh, 2 (smoke)

All internet sites appearing in back matter were available and accurate when this book was sent to press.

Printed in the United States of America.
PA117

TABLE OF CONTENTS

ARRIVING IN AMERICA

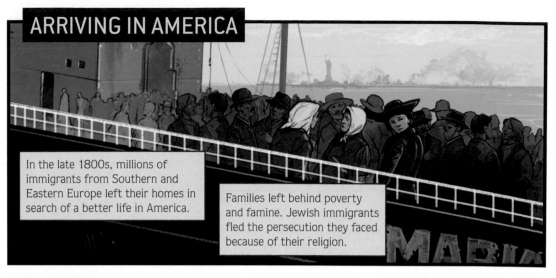

In the late 1800s, millions of immigrants from Southern and Eastern Europe left their homes in search of a better life in America.

Families left behind poverty and famine. Jewish immigrants fled the persecution they faced because of their religion.

Lucio, get upstairs now!

Watch out!

Fish! Fresh fish!

New immigrants discovered a city filled with opportunities and promise.

They also found a city that was crowded and dirty. Many families lived in cramped tenements, which often lacked indoor plumbing.

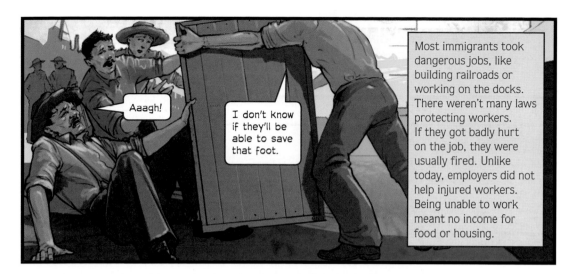

Most immigrants took dangerous jobs, like building railroads or working on the docks. There weren't many laws protecting workers. If they got badly hurt on the job, they were usually fired. Unlike today, employers did not help injured workers. Being unable to work meant no income for food or housing.

Many Italian and Jewish immigrant women found jobs in factories that produced blouses, called shirtwaists.

The factory was hot, crowded, and loud. The women and girls worked long hours. Doors were locked to prevent theft.

It wasn't easy, but the new immigrants hoped that their hard work would lead to a better life.

What on earth is happening, Frances?

I don't know, but it sounds bad.

Frances Perkins was visiting a friend near Washington Square in New York City. The date was March 25, 1911. Around 4:40 p.m., they heard sirens.

I'm going to investigate.

Wait for me!

The Triangle Shirtwaist Factory was on fire.

My sister was on the ninth floor but I can't find her!

The fire started in a bin of fabric and spread through the entire factory within minutes.

We tried to throw water on the fire but the fire hose on the landing didn't work.

The doors were locked from the inside, trapping workers. The rickety fire escape had collapsed.

The fire department's ladders were not tall enough to reach the top floors.

She's going to jump!

No!

If only the owners had listened to our demands.

They have blood on their hands.

This could have been prevented.

7

UPRISING OF THE 20,000

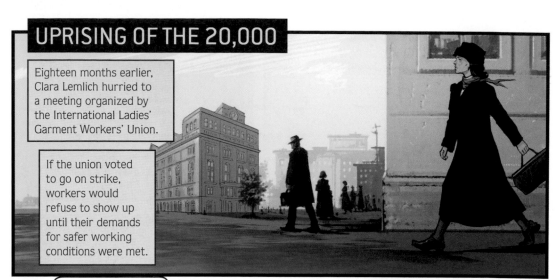

Eighteen months earlier, Clara Lemlich hurried to a meeting organized by the International Ladies' Garment Workers' Union.

If the union voted to go on strike, workers would refuse to show up until their demands for safer working conditions were met.

. . . caution . . .
. . . wait . . .
. . . deliberation . . .

I'm tired of speeches without action.

Clara had been through strikes before. She had been arrested 17 times and even been beaten by men hired by factory owners.

I want to say a few words!

I have listened to the speakers and I have no further patience for talk.

I am one of those who suffers the abuses that have been described.

I am tired of listening to speakers. I move we go on strike!

The crowd cheered its approval for five minutes.

Hear! Hear! Yes!

It's really happening.

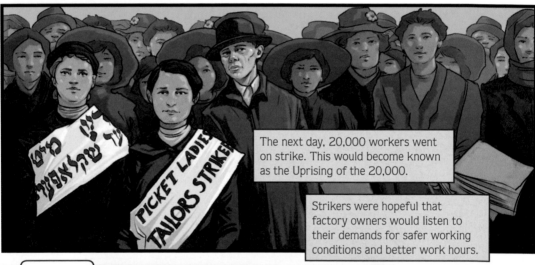

The next day, 20,000 workers went on strike. This would become known as the Uprising of the 20,000.

Strikers were hopeful that factory owners would listen to their demands for safer working conditions and better work hours.

Now they'll have to listen to us.

Clara, you're speaking at 15 union halls today. Rose, we're sending you on a speaking tour of New England to publicize our cause and raise money. We can do this!

Clara Lemlich and her friends, Pauline Newman and Rose Schneiderman, organized the strike.

Factory owners were not happy about the strike.

We're losing money every day the factory sits empty. We need to do something.

This should teach you a lesson!

Some factory owners hired men to harass and attack protestors.

You can't do this! I have a right to protest!

Shut up and get in the cart!

Factory owners also got the police to intimidate and arrest strikers

You are striking against God and Nature, whose law is that man should earn his bread by the sweat of his brow. You are on strike against God!

If we stick together, and we will stick, we will win!

PICKET LADIES
TAILORS STRIKER

PICKET LADIES
TAILORS STRIKER

PICKET LADIES
TAILORS STRIKER

PICKET LADIES
TAILORS STRIKER

Despite these hardships, the strikers were determined to win better working conditions.

Wealthy New York women like Alva Belmont and Anne Morgan heard about the strike and the horrible working conditions in factories. They wanted to help.

On December 5, 1909, Alva Belmont rented the enormous Hippodrome Theatre for a massive rally.

Mayor McClellan was invited but as you see, he did not come. Apparently he wasn't interested in the welfare of 40,000 striking girls.

Alva Belmont invited many city officials to the meeting. None of them showed up.

"We demand equal pay for equal work" "Give women the protection of the vote."

Give the women the vote, so that we may become as powerful as the men are because of their votes.

We'll fight our own battles.

In 1909, women could not vote in the United States. Rally speakers highlighted the importance of giving women the right to vote.

I have been attacked several times by hired men.

Strikers spoke about their experiences on the picket line.

The police dragged me into the courtroom. My boss was there, and he told the judge that I should be deported.

When an officer tried to arrest me, I reminded him that I have a constitutional right to picket!

Daily News

THRONG CHEERS ON THE GIRL STRIKERS

8,000 Gather in the Hippodrome on Mrs. Belmont's Call to Bid Them Triumph

Newspaper accounts of the meeting helped sway public opinion in favor of the strikers.

Anne Morgan hosted a lunch for strike leaders to speak with her wealthy friends.

We want to help. What do you need?

Money to fight with.

Stand beside us on the picket lines. The owners will never pay men to beat us up if you're there.

The women immediately took up a collection and pledged their support to the strikers.

Support workers' rights!

The wealthy women even walked the picket line. They became known as the "mink brigade" because of the expensive furs they wore.

I swear, if they weren't so rich . . .

Quiet! You know we can't touch them now.

The presence of the mink brigade also meant an end to the violence the strikers had experienced on the picket line.

14

But it was the grit and determination of the factory workers themselves that kept the strike going into February 1910.

Most of the factory owners agreed to shorter hours and better pay. In exchange, the workers returned to the factory floors.

Triangle owners Max Blanck and Isaac Harris did not agree to any of the safety conditions the workers wanted.

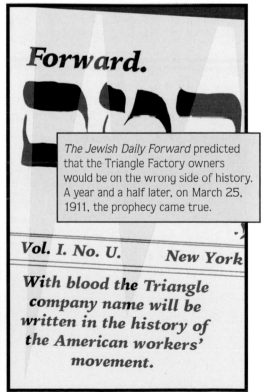

The *Jewish Daily Forward* predicted that the Triangle Factory owners would be on the wrong side of history. A year and a half later, on March 25, 1911, the prophecy came true.

MOURNING

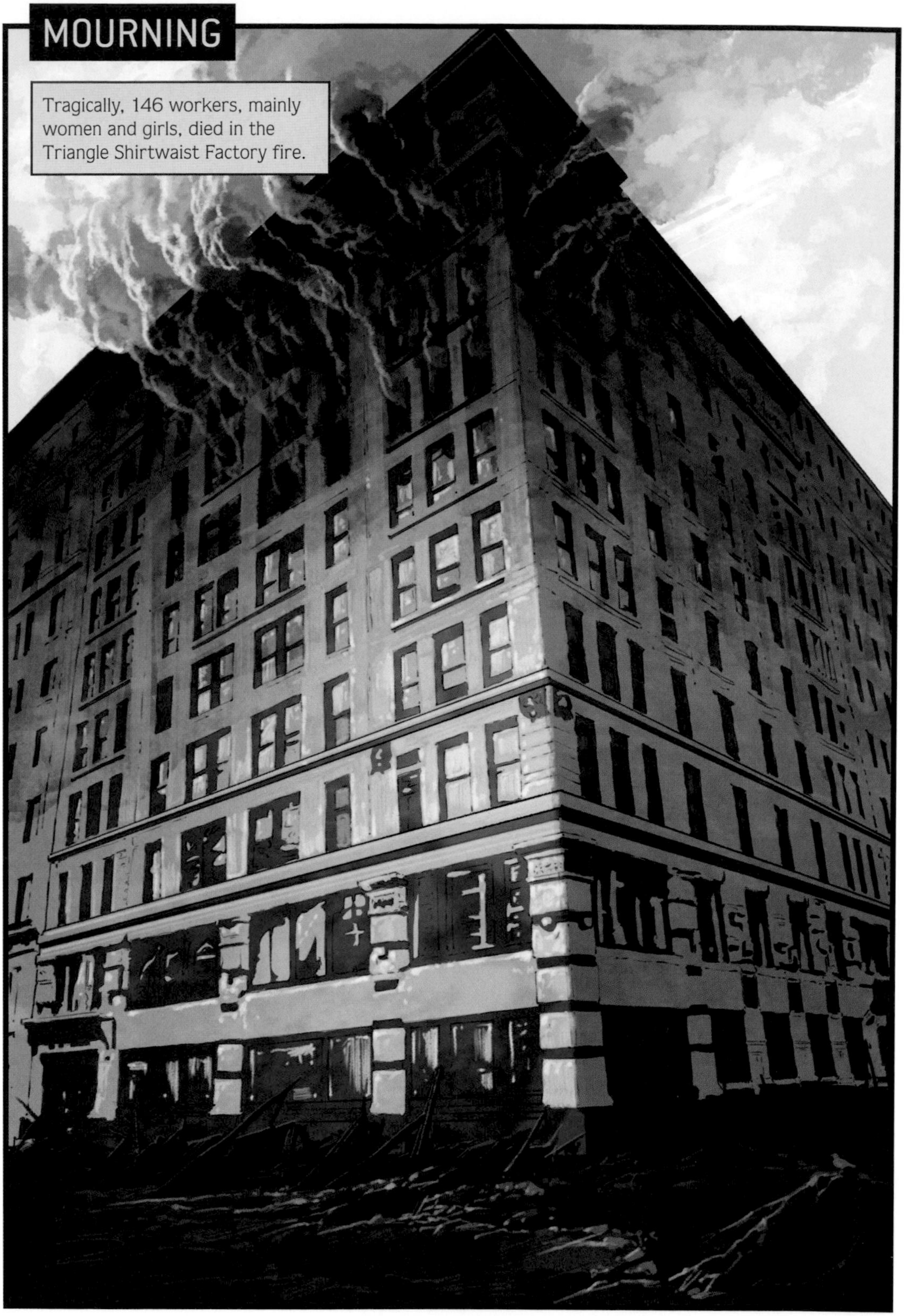
Tragically, 146 workers, mainly women and girls, died in the Triangle Shirtwaist Factory fire.

She was wearing a locket that I gave her for her birthday. Have you seen her?

What will I do without them?

The bodies of the victims were taken to a morgue at Charities Pier. Families searched for loved ones.

So many of my friends died. I can't stand the pain.

Clara Lemlich searched the morgue frantically for a cousin she feared had died.

We worked so hard to make changes. Why didn't all those years of struggle and strike prevent this?

Pauline Newman fell into a deep depression following the news.

I'm tired of resolutions being passed but never acted upon.

Rose Schneiderman lost friends in the fire, too.

On April 2, 1911, Alva Belmont and Anne Morgan organized a meeting to discuss the fire. Around 3,000 people attended.

Everyone wanted to make sure that nothing like the Triangle fire happened again.

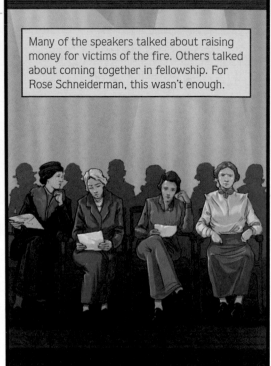

Many of the speakers talked about raising money for victims of the fire. Others talked about coming together in fellowship. For Rose Schneiderman, this wasn't enough.

I would be a traitor to those poor burned bodies if I were to come here to talk good fellowship.

This is not the first time girls have been burned alive in this city. Every week I must learn of the untimely death of one of my sister workers.

Every time we strike, the factory owners and police are allowed to attack us.

I know from experience it is up to the working people to save themselves. And the only way is through a strong working-class movement!

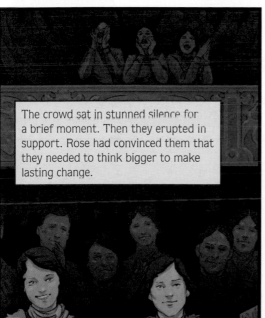

The crowd sat in stunned silence for a brief moment. Then they erupted in support. Rose had convinced them that they needed to think bigger to make lasting change.

The crowd voted to send a Committee on Safety to Albany, New York, the state capital.

Frances Perkins was named to the committee.

But first, the city mourned. Funeral processions wound through the narrow streets as families buried their dead.

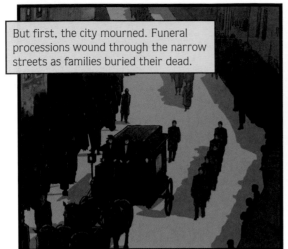

Some families, like the Malteses, the Brenmans, and the Saracinos, lost multiple family members in the fire.

I can't believe they're both gone.

We need to honor them and everyone who died.

The International Ladies' Garment Workers' Union organized a public funeral procession to lay six unidentified bodies to rest.

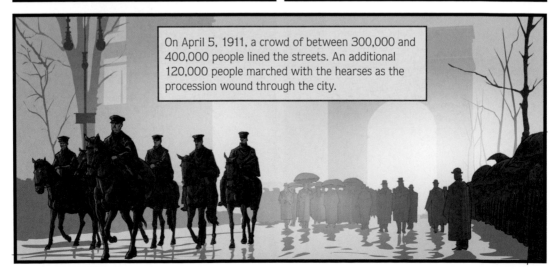

On April 5, 1911, a crowd of between 300,000 and 400,000 people lined the streets. An additional 120,000 people marched with the hearses as the procession wound through the city.

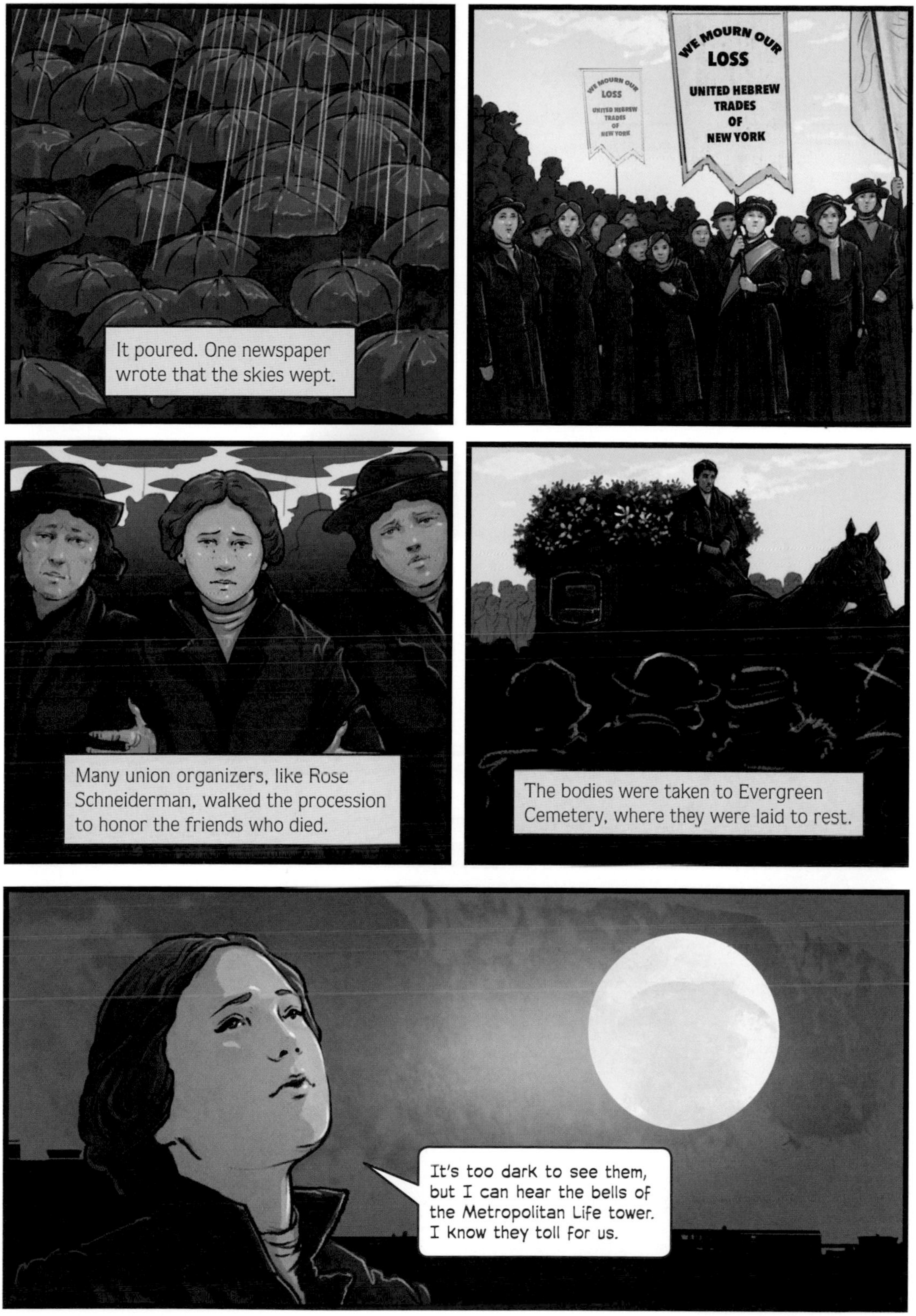
It poured. One newspaper wrote that the skies wept.
WE MOURN OUR LOSS
UNITED HEBREW TRADES OF NEW YORK
Many union organizers, like Rose Schneiderman, walked the procession to honor the friends who died.
The bodies were taken to Evergreen Cemetery, where they were laid to rest.
It's too dark to see them, but I can hear the bells of the Metropolitan Life tower. I know they toll for us.

MAKING LASTING CHANGES

I'm afraid the committee won't get anywhere. Tammany Hall doesn't want it.

A few weeks after the funeral march, Frances Perkins ran into New York State Representative Al Smith at a train station.

Tammany Hall was a political organization that controlled New York politics.

Why not? Don't they care?

They don't like any committee that they can't control.

So what do we do?

There's not much you can do. If Tammany Hall doesn't want the committee to succeed, it won't.

The state assembly formed a commission to investigate factory safety. But few people thought the commission would make any lasting changes. Until . . .

Sir, we should rethink the factory safety commission.

If we throw our support behind a working-class movement, think of all the votes we can get from factory workers.

Fine. Tammany Hall will support the commission.

On June 30, 1911, Governor Dix signed a law that created the Factory Investigating Commission. The Commission would investigate factories in New York's nine largest cities.

Frances Perkins finally believed they could improve workplace safety and workers' rights.

Clara Lemlich, Frances Perkins, Rose Schneiderman, and Pauline Newman all joined the Factory Investigating Committee as investigators.

Commission members visited factories across New York State. They found the same conditions that led to the deadly Triangle fire.

The fire escape doesn't even reach the ground!

Only an acrobat could use it.

Look at all that fabric piled on the floor! That's why Triangle burned so quickly.

Not a single sprinkler to be seen.

These doors are locked too.

The Commission also held public hearings.

At the factory, there's one toilet in the middle of the room, and it's only flushed once a day.

We eat lunch at the same table where we have been working. The table is dirty, and no one cleans it.

In one canning factory, Commission members saw children as young as five years old working alongside their parents.

How long do the children work?

Until they pass out from exhaustion.

The Factory Investigating Commission transformed workplaces in New York. They passed laws that improved fire safety, ventilation, and sanitation.

LEGACY OF THE TRIANGLE FIRE

In a 1964 speech, Frances Perkins reflected on the legacy of the Triangle fire.

The fire made a terrible impression on the people of the State of New York. I can't begin to tell you how disturbed the people were everywhere.

The Factory Investigating Commission seems in some way to have paid the debt society owed to those children who died in the fire.

It's their contribution that we have this really magnificent series of legislative acts to protect and improve the law regarding the protection of work people.

The Triangle fire still influences us today. We have fire sprinklers . . .

. . . fire drills . . .

. . . and safe fire escapes because of Triangle.

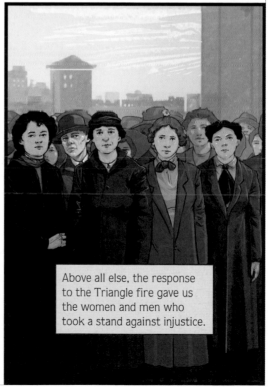

Above all else, the response to the Triangle fire gave us the women and men who took a stand against injustice.

MORE ABOUT THE FIGHT FOR WORKERS' RIGHTS

Although they fled many hardships in their homelands, Jewish and Italian women faced new barriers after immigrating to America. For most immigrants—male and female—it was hard to find jobs that were not dangerous. Recent immigrants lacked the education levels and fluency in English to find safer, higher paying jobs.

Women faced strong pressures to stop working outside the house in favor of getting married and having children. They also faced discrimination in the clothing factories, where the higher paying jobs were mainly given to men. Even within the unions themselves, men held most of the leadership positions.

The Uprising of the 20,000 was important because of the leadership of women. Women organized, encouraged, and supported each other as they fought for better working conditions. They stood strong against the factory owners, the police, and the courts, which were trying to bring them down.

These women also found allies among more powerful women, like the mink brigade, to help advance their cause. Their work is an important example of the power of collective bargaining and unions in fighting for workers' rights.

Women organizers also made sure that those who died in the Triangle Shirtwaist Factory fire didn't die in vain. Their actions led to lasting impact. Laws were changed to protect workers, first in New York State and then across the nation.

In 1933 Frances Perkins became Secretary of Labor under President Franklin Delano Roosevelt. In that role, she continued to reform workplace safety. Workers were allowed to unionize and advocate for their rights. Workweeks were shortened. Children were kept from having to work full time and in dangerous conditions. We have women like Clara Lemlich, Rose Schneiderman, and others to thank for these rights.

GLOSSARY

collective bargaining (kuh-LEK-tiv BAR-guhn-ing)—discussions between an employer and a group of employees usually on wages, hours, and working conditions

immigration (im-uh-GRAY-shuhn)—an act or instance of coming into a foreign country to live

mink (MINGK)—a small mammal often farmed for its pelt for use in coats and wraps

morgue (MORG)—a place where dead bodies are kept until they are identified or released for burial

negotiate (ni-GOH-shee-ate)—to bargain or discuss something to come to an agreement

persecution (pur-si-KYOO-shuhn)—cruel or unfair treatment, often because of race or religious beliefs

poverty (PAH-vuhr-tee)—the state of being poor or without money

shirtwaist (SHIRT-wayst)—type of blouse with a tight waist, high neck, and puffy sleeves popular in the early 1900s

state assembly (STAYT uh-SEM-blee)—the lower house of the New York State Legislature

suffrage (SUHF-rij)—the right to vote

tenement (TEN-uh-muhnt)—a rundown apartment building, especially one that is crowded and in a poor part of a city

union (YOON-yuhn)—an organized group of workers that tries to gain better pay and working conditions for workers

ventilation (ven-tuh-LAY-shuhn)—a system that allows the flow of fresh air